# GLASSWORKS

David Wojahn
# GLASSWORKS

University of Pittsburgh Press

Published by the University of Pittsburgh Press, Pittsburgh, Pa. 15260
Copyright © 1987, David Wojahn
All rights reserved
Feffer and Simons, Inc., London
Manufactured in the United States of America


Library of Congress Cataloging in Publication Data

Wojahn, David, 1953–
 Glassworks.

 (Pitt poetry series)
 I. Title.  II. Series.
PS3573.044G5  1987      811'.54      86-25036
ISBN 0-8229-3553-8
ISBN 0-8229-5389-7 (pbk.)

Acknowledgment is made to the following publications where some of these poems
appeared, often in earlier versions: *The Agni Review* ("*Les Enfants du Paradis*"); *The
American Scholar* ("The Truth"); *The Antioch Review* (" 'Satin Doll' "); *The Black
Warrior Review* ("*The World of Donald Evans*"); *Crazyhorse* ("Particular Words" and
"Song of Burning"); *The Georgia Review* ("250 Bradford"); *The Missouri Review* ("The
Last Couples Leaving the Green Dolphin Bar," "Lot's Wife," and "Porch Lights"); *New
England Review and Bread Loaf Quarterly* ("Dates, for Example" and "Santorini"); *North
American Review* ("Steam"); *Ploughshares* ("The Bicycle" and "Dark-House Spearing");
*Poetry* ("Glassworks at Saratoga," "Pentecost," and "This Moment"); *The Poetry Miscel-
lany* ("Blitz, London, 1944" and "Riding the Empire Builder, 1948"); *The Reaper*
("Little Orgonon"); *Sewanee Review* ("The Third Language"); *Sonora Review* ("The
Paris Cinema"); *Tar River Poetry* ("The Anniversary"); *Tendril* ("Cool Nights of
October"); *Telescope* ("This Journey on Bach's Birthday"); and *Virginia Quarterly
Review* ("Census" and "Past the Dark Arroyo").

"A Game of Croquet" was published first in *Grand Street*. "The Bicycle," "Cool Nights of
October," and " 'Satin Doll' " also appeared in the anthology *New American Poets of the
Eighties* (Wampeter Press). "Dark-House Spearing" was reprinted in *The Ploughshares
Reader: Poetry for the Eighties* (Ploughshare Books).

I would like to thank the National Endowment for the Arts and the Fine Arts Work Center
in Provincetown for fellowships which helped me to complete this collection.

*The publication of this book is supported by grants
from the National Endowment for the Arts
in Washington, D.C., a Federal agency,
and the Pennsylvania Council on the Arts.*

For Lynda Hull

*"It is the same in life; the heart changes,*
*and it is our worst sorrow."*

—Proust

# CONTENTS

## I

## II

# CONTENTS

## III

I

1st section about
losses?

# SATIN DOLL

It's probably the year her marriage
fails, though the photo, blackened now
on the edges of its sepia, doesn't say:
my aunt on the hood of the blue Chevy coupe,

straw hat and summer dress. It's the year
she carries the novels and notebooks
into the backyard to burn them, and when she finishes
her dress and apron are covered with ashes, rising

in what she wants to call a pillar of fire
but it is only smoke on a damp day.
She walks back to the house and her first
sickly daughter, feeling the one

inside her kick. She thinks of going
back to her maiden name, and the daughter
cries in her crib like the passionless
wind up the St. Croix River bluffs.

And when she was a child there, the day
of the grade school picnic, they found
a woman drowned on the banks. Everyone stared
and no one closed the eyes staring back.

But now it's raining on the first spring night
of 1947, six years to my birth,
and I don't want to leave her here. I want
the kitchen radio to murmur

some slithering big band and "Satin Doll"
from the Casablanca ballroom, high in Chicago's clouds.
I want her to see the women floating
in their taffeta, chilly red corsages from

their pencil-mustached men, ivory tuxedos, lotion,
and bay rum. She can almost touch them now. Duke Ellington
rises from the sprawling Steinway as the four
trombones begin their solo, horns glittering

under the spinning globe of mirrors. And now
she's dancing, isn't she? Until the cupboards shake,
until the window, already trembling with rain,
hums its vibrato, and she's holding herself in her arms

so tightly she can feel the veins
in her shoulders throb to their separate music,
until this is a song she can dance with too,
and I can let her go.

# STARLINGS

          As if the tree itself
were straining to fly off,
          peppering the branches,
               the hiss of shuffled cards,
          until they're more than she
can bear. Earthbound, shouting,
          in her nightgown she stumbles
               out with a spoon, a lobster pot

          to fend them off, though always
they return, until by sundown
          nothing disturbs their sleep,
               derision so absolute
          she's weeping in the porch light's
yellow arc, the evening
          choked with them. I wake
               to spy her from my room,

          the noise like tin-roof rain.
Probably she's drunk
          again. It's probably a night
               my father is two thousand
          miles away, unloading
on some Indian reservation
          mailsacks from a baggage car.
               I know she'll stay awake

all night. I'll rise again
at five—the clock face's radium
    shimmer—then creep into
        the livingroom, where finally
    she's bowed her head,
her romance fallen open
    on the carpet, the pages
        trembling in the morning breeze.

    Outside, they're waking too,
their *sh sh sh* a sound
    at first I think is meant
        to quiet us. I want to slither
    into her lap. I want to be
the book she reads, before the noise
    begins to deafen us, before
        she wakes and never sleeps again.

# DARK-HOUSE SPEARING

In my father's red sweater
I wake to snow in the South.
His first vacation alone,
he's sleeping this week on my sofa,

says again we never owned a yellow Olds.
But I remember him
in his only suit,
leaving for the doctor in St. Paul,

1956, shoveling snow from the wheels
of the yellow car:
the memory
from which I date the world.

We have learned the balm
of trivial disagreement,
though he doesn't believe in words.
We eat breakfast

at a restaurant window,
the river murky with ice.
Because his brother,
ten years younger, died last month

in alcoholic coma,
he doesn't want talk, just company.
So even here I mention snow,
the absence of color

from the interplay
of many colors.
He tells me I will never understand
the real simplicity of things.

∫

So I remember dark-house spearing,
Christmas in the fifties.
We walked across the bay
at Lake Millacs,

the flashlight glowing
by the circle we cut.
Fish swim curious,
illegal toward the light.

Dozens come. I'm five.
Father raises his grandfather's spear,
sunfish and smallmouth swarm like bees.
Dark-house spearing,

Minnesota's sheer
December ice-mist around us.
I tell him how I woke
from the dream again last night,

of fish alive and trembling in the bag
I clutch riding home on his shoulders.
Sunrise. My uncle stands
at the window of my childhood home

and father and I are singing,
floating toward the light.
Useless to remember it, he says,
when you have the details wrong.

∫

*direct address*

I have the details wrong.
Father, I wanted to evoke for you
words beyond the absence of words,
so wholly it would be enough

**8**

to cause us to begin again.
Weeping, you told me
you could not remember
your last words with your brother.

Daily, father, I wait
for the real simplicity of things.
Sometimes, when I shut my eyes,
I'm back in ashen fields,

steel-colored sky.
My hands cling to the cedar fence
you said would hold
the snow back from the world.

1956—I know already
snow will win, swirl in the living rooms,
all night drift
against the beds and windows.

And those who rise at dawn,
rubbing the night from their eyes,
none of them will understand
what they wake to or what they have lost.

snow represents an absence —death?
ultimate simplicity

# THE TRUTH

*—after Jarrell*

This afternoon I brought him a toy dog.
He asked me its name and soon
we were weeping in each other's arms,
and I loved him again, though he wasn't himself.
That's what the nurse said, too. *He's so very small,*
she said, *to look so old.*
The ward was drab. The children
all wore lime green hospital gowns.
But he wasn't sick, only hurt past recognition.

Now I watch the winter fields
pass like memory from beyond the train,
nothing green. In the window I can see myself
through a girl on a plain of snow
schooling a pony in an oblong pen,
or a boy on a hill watching cars
unraveling light on the road to Derry.
Evening now, jigsaws of smoke from the chimneys.
With her riding crop, the girl
conducts crescendos of snow. She's the age
my daughter would have been. She looks up—
the sirens of the rail crossing.

Across from me, the old woman snores,
Christmas chocolates and a hatbox on her lap.
The conductor wakes her
to say that London nears. Tonight,
no blackout, no searchlights in the sky.
My husband is not in Scotland, my children
not asleep, and I am not
the mother of the son I love. Arriving here
beneath the smoked glass dome of the station,
the atmosphere is steam, and nothing
stays the same.

**10**

*Blitz* they called it. I didn't know
where Gerald was, and when the roof
exploded like a paper sack, I kept shaking Sarah
until the life seemed gone from both of us.
The boy stood watching from the corner.

It happens so fast. You look up
and your life is changed past recognition.
Though today I put my arms around him
and we cried, for a moment he was not my son.
I wanted to shout to the nurse
and everyone there was some mistake.
Yet he was all I had,
not himself, and we cried.

watching

11

# THE THIRD LANGUAGE

I want to talk about the harbor lights
but first a wind beneath the door,
chilling the tiles, the slippers.
A single window, he's newly arrived.
The harbor is not picturesque, my grandfather
neither tall nor striking. No one speaks German
in the port of Boston. He has fled

the Kaiser's army, his family of officers,
though he understands the Morse Code,
knows there's a future in telegraphy.
So the harbor lights blink white code
in a language he is still to learn.
The bluefish he fries in a pungent batter—
beer, smoked cheese, garlic cloves.

You're used to better than this. Grandfather,
they will burn your Midwestern house,
the night you tap out Wilson's declaration
of war, in a station I saw torn down
when I was five, tap, tap it in code,
your third language, that somewhere
predicts meningitis, that says

how for years my mother will see
your ghost at her bedside, the buttons
invisibly pulled from her dresses
and left on the tables and chairs
of your widow's house. Three longs,
four shorts, three longs again . . .
And I'm addressing you, the message partial.

Tonight the tile is cold on my feet,
my view the lights of a city below.
As I write, you carve the steaming filet,
complain the batter's too salty.
You watch the pier's red beacons
from a window starred with frost.

In the third language, we're aware
and unaware. But sometimes I lose                    keys, typewriter
the buttons of my shirts, find them
in cupboards and drawers, disturb my neighbors
late with typing. A ringing in my ears.          memory
The smell of garlic, the bluefish frying.

# BLITZ, LONDON, 1944

*sonnet* —

He's met the girl only once before, to share
a Guinness with her in a pub. He let her show
him pictures of her parents' graves, the legless brother
who wakes each night from mumbled dreams of Anzio:
she shares the parents' flat with him. And no, she said,
my father could not meet her there, or anywhere.
"To hell with you Yanks." But now they meet again inside
the cavern of the Tube, sirens, and the loosened plaster
flickering like snow on them. Thronging with
six hundred others, they touch but scarcely speak,
and soon she's dozing on his shoulder, the hiss
of ack-ack fire above, until the all-clear sounds. She wakes
to dust the plaster from her hair. She shakes his hand.
*Such a lonely man,* she thinks, *such an ugly lonely man.*

*switch of viewpoint*

*sonnet — rhymes*

# RIDING THE EMPIRE BUILDER, 1948

My father in the snowy window, face incandescent
And the sky all day going on with its labors
Like a man throwing mailsacks from a train, long descent
From Whitefish to the plains, and in the corner
Of his eye he can only see steam, engine straining
Away from Badlands to the Minnesota border,
And it snows all the way from Fergus Falls, staining
The landscape to bone, until the scene is ordered
Around the orange glow of his Camel, the stove
And its butane purr, and the last hundred miles
He dozes on a mailsack, chamois work gloves,
The Browning automatic on the table, aisle upon aisle
Of mail, and here a stranger's coffin bound express
For where he's going too, crossed hands drowsing on his chest.

15

# COOL NIGHTS OF OCTOBER

I wanted to spare you this, the lying alone,
    the moon as it rises,
        watery and diffuse

like a washcloth pressed to the forehead
    of a girl so still she can barely breathe.
        I read of her now on page

four hundred and seventy-eight.
    I've wakened in the TV's bluish light
        and the noise my neighbor

the one-eyed Cuban makes,
    sharpening a stick against the sidewalk.
        He wears the battered face I saw last week

above the gate of St. Louis Cemetery—
    a marble angel with a broken trumpet.
        In the dampness after rain

it had no eyes or forehead.
    On page four hundred and seventy-nine
        Turgenev lets the girl die. The mother

had been reading to her, a novel in French.
    Turgenev does not tell us how the woman
        drops her book, cups her daughter's face

and cries out softly. The death scene,
    like Bazarov's, is unsentimental.
        These are the first cool nights of October.

The Cuban beats his wife. I hear them
    over car horns and Samba records,
        the spas of Baden-Baden, the roulette tables,

the calculating Russian gentry. Turgenev
   was fat and lived alone. His brain
      is in the *Guinness Book,*

having weighed nearly seven pounds.
   Ivan Turgenev, I am David Wojahn
      and some nights I can't sleep.

I read of you in English
   and tire of the word and heavy mind.
      I wanted to spare you. A mother weeps

beside a still, consumptive daughter
   and some angelic Cuban, his eye patch askew,
      strikes his wife again across the face.

**17**

# THE PARIS CINEMA

Here, the images repeat themselves more restlessly
than in better films, everything indulgent and removed.
A woman, gold teeth, goes down on three tattooed men

forlornly in a sham of lust. It has nothing
to do with nuance, which is said to be the secret
of truly making love. It's all men here, heads bowed

as if lust were a too-demanding occupation,
and now they're tired of it. Simple plots,
where every character is gratified, and usually a dozen

couples fuck themselves a little listlessly
to some improbable grand finale. You might say
you come here because you're lonely, and even this too-bright

semblance of touch will help. But you're the only lover
these images remind you of. Numb, you leave the theater
for the darkening street—your eyes don't need

to adjust. In this Southern port town,
warm and marshy as Alexandria, you think of Cavafy's window,
a single candle, sultry apartment above a bordello.

And Cavafy gazing through his pipe smoke to the full
kinetic street below, the boyish faces he longs for.
He recalls a face from thirty years past,

the summer of 1903, and he turns the face to words
formed carefully on yellow paper, and now he's breathing hard,
the hot night drifting off, his longing almost soothed.

# THIS MOMENT

And then one morning the light has changed,
the window troubled with rain, and you think,
for a moment, the light will never change again.
The red oaks scatter their little veins

of fire to the street, littering the cars,
and you stare at your hands as if
they held unfathomable secrets, like the girl
in Hopper's *New York Movie*, blonde head bowed,

her usher's coat and slacks, the yellow
EXIT light above her. You've pinned the girl
to your wall and watched her for weeks,
want her to instruct you

daily in the postures of solitude. Last night,
alone in an unfamiliar city, you read again
Keats's final letters—all he saw
of Rome his balcony window, and a room

that held so much of his dying
its contents were later burned.
*Thank God it has come,* he said,
and seemed, wrote his friend, to sleep.

When you shut the book, shaken and far from your life,
you were afraid to speak, even to yourself,
afraid this moment could never pass.
Afternoons, you run your miles

in the park to lose yourself, the way,
one drunken night in Venice,
you tried and failed to be lost—alley walls
your outstretched arms encompassed,

staggering thin canals, streetlights
glistening oily on the water
where you try to find your image.
*Our ties to ourselves,* wrote Keats, *so tenuous*

*I think they break without our knowing it.*
So these are the days you enter. Touched carefully—
the trembling hands of your blind students
tracing your forehead and neck.

This sting, and your neighbor burning leaves,
his face a wavering blur through smoke.
And your own face, suddenly ghostly
as you scrape away the ten-year-old beard,

clumps falling red, red to the sink,
this face of someone
whose eyes could be yours, who nods
or turns away.

**20**

# CENSUS

Because they were new here, and most of them
afraid of deportation, the families didn't understand
their obligation to have names
or to know where they had lived

on April 1 five years before.
I used my Spanish badly, like a child
making drawings with crayons
to almost explain—government forms, the law.

Arizona in July, they kept their doors
and windows closed, the insides fanless,
from modesty, or fear. Once, in a house
no larger than my kitchen,

I documented twenty-five, some whose names
the coughing *abuella*
forgot and asked me to invent. For a time
the work let me leave myself,

though I'm sorry it came down to only that—
you left the marriage for Italy and Greece,
and for weeks I spoke to no one
but the dog with a cast on her leg,

the weary Sonorans who feared me.
A landlord used his pass key to let me in
to the trailer of a grocery clerk no one had counted.
Dead six days, he'd been clipping his nails

with scissors when the heart attack came.
Weeks I dreamed of him, and tried to find
the mathematics for all these losses,
how few things add up, how finally we stand

befuddled as those Amazon tribes
who keep their system small and terrible,
a number for *one*, a number for *two*,
a final number for *many*.

||

# A GAME OF CROQUET

—*after Eakins*

The boats pull out
though many will be lost to
the storm unleashed tonight, hurricane winds
of the century's first autumn, but for now
the world is strict bright
colors on a lawn,

a girl singing
the advanced songs of Mahler
at a window where the curtains stir only
to the notes cascading from her lips,
the stricken fall only
with the *clack*

of maple globes
against one another, moribund
planets in collision, though I suppose
these minute deaths mean something beyond
themselves, Katherine in her
pink gingham dress,

gathered at the waist,
Mavis in simple white; and their
suitor, Captain Shuttleworth, returned last
month from Havana, peers from the gazebo's
botched minaret to a thundercloud
simmering above

Hyannisport, the bay
a gunmetal blue, the wind now rising
as Dottie the maid gathers picnic baskets,
overturned goblets, the ladies' magazines from
London, calling the airedales
home; and the game

is won by Mavis
who takes Captain Shuttleworth's
arm in triumph, as though she has now proven
he will choose her, leaving Katherine to sulk
her afternoons along the paths
of the salt marsh

where gulls wheel
down to the brackish water.
Accompany her, please. Touch her forehead
that glistens with fever, the trembling, girlish
shoulders. She feels as though
she will never die.

# THE LAST COUPLES LEAVING
# THE GREEN DOLPHIN BAR

Because it was the end of summer
the red moon caught in skittish treetops

and our  bodies made a kind of speech          gesture
like breaking glass, far off.

The young Chicano men
turned radios up loud outside.

You stayed up late to read
detective stories in the broken chair,

white rum sweating on the tablecloth,
a towel on your head and the loose,

printed robe from Marrakesh.
Because it was the end of summer,

the only rains since April skimmed
the red tile roofs and empty lots,

falling on those couples from the Green Dolphin Bar,
four hundred miles from ocean,

who set their mugs and glasses down
and cast their shadows on our bedroom wall.

They made their paths
unsteadily toward home and slept,

unsurprised by anything. At the windowsill,
after you could finally rest, I'd watch them

in the evening's dreamy undertow,
not thinking how the smallest detail

changes memory to distance. Didn't you stir then,
troubling the sheets until,

from sleep, you asked who called your name?
Even then, it was not too late.

# PORCH LIGHTS

drill their yellow holes in evening
and where you walk

*2nd person*

the houses go on drifting with their cargo.
You've tried to sleep, but now you find your image

gleaming from the puddled sidewalk water,
the pay phone's light. You hold

each other's gaze, but you know it's just
your face, know this isolation doesn't scare,

though you wanted, simply,
to glimpse another life, the way new lovers do,

*pov's 1st person into 3rd*

even when they dress so shyly in the morning.
Remember them? They ate breakfast on a porch

in Maine, secretly ashamed of loneliness,
how the whole intoxicating mess

began again the night before.
This is why the woman's fingers

turned her napkin into flakes of snow,
why the man would think of houses

floating dully with their loads
and watch a young dalmatian

penned inside a neighbor's yard. It howled
and wound its leash around a tree,

its radius a little smaller.

29

# SANTORINI

From the cliffside and its bone-colored town, you zigzagged
with the others down the stairs, past German tourists
on their mules, for the ferry to the sleeping volcano.
Beside the abandoned jail for petty thieves and
political prisoners, partially demolished by the new regime,
you sat with them to watch a sputtering, prewar biplane
skywrite a message in Greek, until the letters blurred.
Why remember this more clearly than the famous light,
White as radium, or the sea, delft blue, circling itself
like courtroom testimony? For weeks you'd wakened

every night past two, swearing that your intricate
self-consciousness was criminal, trying to remember
the dream you knew had frightened you. You traveled that month
with a British couple, their arguments sharp
and unpredictable. They came from Manchester and the woman
told you she was dying, "a rebellion in the blood," her hair
thin stubble beneath her scarves. But the man, after their trip,
intended to divorce her: "The unfaithfulness,
the bickering. . . . What else to do?" So he drank without her
until the tavernas closed, and you'd sleep with her

in the C class room the three of you shared, windows jutting
to a terrace where sheets and checkered tablecloths
wavered on a line. She spoke, sometimes, of desire,
which she called a man and woman going home
to separate flats, to wash themselves from each other
at metal sinks, ceramic bidets, their lives now shorter
by an hour or two. When you'd enter her, she'd give a cry
you thought was pain, though you told yourself her story
was a lie, and her death seemed less important than
the fissures of your own confusion, and the hatred

of yourself you felt for thinking this, so far from home
in a room where Sylvester Stallone, and the Botticelli
*Annunciation*, leered down from calendars above the broken
director's chair. She'd chain smoke and describe the job
she'd had to quit, a cosmetics company. Later, you'd walk
with her to the village below, together lug
her husband to his bed, where he talked in his sleep
all night like a man being covered with a rain of ashes.
You'd comfort her with practiced glibness, and once she told you
you spoke like the guide that morning on the tour,

leaning above the crater, adjusting his tie, then hissing
his empty rhetoric—how twenty thousand Therans perished,
how the fire-rain and ash entombed their city,
bread still in ovens, meals still laid. *And this volcano,*
*millenia later, slumbers like a hibernating animal.*
His hands dribble pumice, black chips like coins.
Abstractedly he whispers, as if the phrases,
whose meaning he still does not perceive,
he had over and over rehearsed before a mirror,
watching his lips move, plotting his manic gestures.

# SONG OF THE BURNING

—*Jim Morrison*

I wanted the heart to scream.
I wanted the sound of chalk on a blackboard,
shrillness and pain
still echoing from childhood, another way

to talk around love.
I wanted it steady, pulsing of light
from a distant star, the Bo Diddley *thunk*
of drum and bass, the organ
crescendoing. *Who do you love? Who
do you love?* I wanted song without story,
only the cruelest metaphor. But who
finally gives a shit?
The body runs down.
Love turns to habit, and some nights you wail
or meth yourself past forgetting.
This is why you think some nights
you're Satan's poor facsimile, and why

you'll wake up dead one morning.
*Talk around love:* I mean that,
until love's all spell and incantation,
a name like GLORIA, and you sound
each letter out like need,
or show your cock to half the wasted
little punks of Miami, the strobes
all over you like hands.
In my dream, someone makes a movie

beginning with my song: first you see a jungle
resurrect to yellow flame, rise up
like outstretched arms. On
and on it burns until you'd think
the leaves themselves were howling.
*This is the end,* I'm singing,
*beautiful friend, my only friend,*
*the flames want to wrap us*
*all in their hands,* and that's
when I know what love is,
perfectly. Then maybe the band
gets projected on the screen, playing tighter
than they've ever been, and we've all
got those bleeding
flaming hearts of Mexican Christs.
We all understand where we're going.
And you all know, you poor dumb fuckers,

what you have to do to follow me.
It's the fifth of July, 1971, and I wake
in the best *pensione* in Paris. 4:00 A.M.
I start the day with speedball,
spoon a puddle of flame. Seven floors
below my window, a dwarf on crutches sells
the first edition of *Le Figaro.*

A couple walks arm in arm toward him,
a black guy, Algerian maybe,
the girl with straight blonde hair.
The black guy strokes
her ass as she buys the paper.
She points at something
in the air above them, as all the neon lights
in the city flicker off.

At hours like this you understand
there were songs you were never
able to write, Song Of The Burning,
Song Of Revelation, Song
That Is Past Forgetting.
At hours like this you rise
to address the ages, history,
the universe. You poor dumb bastards,

I swear you'll never hear my voice again.

# GLASSWORKS AT SARATOGA

*—in memory of James L. White*

He cut his throat, the millionaire,
while shaving when his private rail car
was rammed by a freight behind it.
He lies with his wife near the racetrack
and abandoned bottleworks, SPENCER TRASK
toppled and spray-painted green.

I brought your book here, Jim,
where tourists sift through yellow strata
and glass slag for colonial bottles. Sometimes
it's enough to find a fragment:
this one's smoky glass, the letters OGA
like an aphasic's sentence, or the water glass
I used once, broken, to cut my wrist
when a woman left. I saved it wrapped
in tissue in my desk drawer for a year.

With a metal detector, a woman scans the dirt for coins.
The couple swigging vodka on the station wagon hood
take their blanket to a better spot. Another month
beyond your death begins. Another city
where I've tacked your last photo above my desk,
cheeks all shadow, frayed white sweater against
the mossy apartment bricks,
its weight all that holds you there.

For a moment I am back with you
and Tess in Minneapolis, that final Saturday,
the guttering restaurant light
where you whisper Vallejo—the stoical frost
that shined in him, the ruby-colored rope
that creaked inside his body made him laugh,

sometimes, to himself. But when
his final fever came in Paris
because it had dwelled in him for years,
because the Spanish Republic was also
dying, no poetry came back to him.

And today, because the sky has wanted
to rain all morning, but now gives up, goes numb,
then blue, I hold my jigsaw of glass to light,
rub it on the scar. Spencer Trask
must have stood amazed, the red gush
on his shaving hand, pearl-handled razor
dropping open on the floor. Jim, because today
I am far from your death, let me
be far from my own. I used to think
the dead have vivid dreams. I know better now.

# LOT'S WIFE

Narrow white streets,
    the iron gate. With her husband
        she follows the angel who floats

like fire, who soon will ignite
    with his blue troubled eyes
        the city she knows best—

her friends who bicker in the crowded
    bazaar, precarious vessels
        balanced on their heads.

And her husband, the dark veins
    of his forehead throbbing,
        how does he converse with a being

made wholly of light? Up the goat path
    rimming the town, foothalls with their winter
        mantle of rust, she wants to touch

the raiments of the angel, there
    below the elbow, the way she would touch
        her husband on the days

she sees him as a stranger, whispering to him
    *I am here,* as if she could lose herself
        in the furrows of his otherness.

She wheels back now
    at who she was—a landscape of flame.
        *Who is this man I have known*

*so long, his eyes possessed*
    *by the god who conspires with him,*
        *for whom I've abandoned myself?*

And the seizure of transformation,
    the single spasm
        that rivets her to earth,

the salt-taste for an instant in her mouth,
    then the taste,
        undecipherable, of nothing.

The angel with his fiery palm
    now shades the husband's eyes,
        blinded by

the whiteness before them,
    the purity, bitter and dry,
        of the saved.

# STEAM

The cloud pulled its smoky sleeves across
the mountain, where Christ in cement,
seventy feet tall and throbbing
His orange airplane beacon, gestured to the Ozarks,
His benediction lost in fog.
We drank champagne on the hotel balcony,
tossed the plastic glasses down
into the ravine below, watching the Savior's
arm weave in and out of mist. I want to say
you rose from the deck chair to whisper my name,

and massage my forehead like a warm wind
dragging the evening behind. But already
I knew you'd turn back to our room
and in the gold leaf oval of the mirror
press your trembling head against
its steamy face. Then, as if to no one:
*There are so many things*
*I can't understand.* You faced me and I saw
the long red mark from the mirror
crosshatching your cheek. You slept, and all afternoon

I wandered over cobbled alleys in the rain,
path overgrown to the mines, mineral baths abandoned
half a century, tin-roofed company shacks.
I remembered the Belgian doctor from the 1890s
and the baths he prepared here
for burn victims and lepers, who came
from everywhere. With his white-smocked
assistants, he'd lower them with silken ropes
into water that churned out
boiling from the mountain. The idea

was to burn them twice, exhaust their pain
into simple numbness. The cure, he wrote,
is admitting no cure. The echoes of their cries,
clear summer nights, could be heard by passengers
of trains far across the valley.
Those nights you'd wake, crying for
a lover who was dead, I wanted
to merge your sorrow with my own,
as if pain could modify
pain into love, or wisdom,

and when you raised yourself in sleep
from the brass hotel room bed and called
someone else's name, I felt I was lowering you
into water so hot I could only
see steam, and your cries for him,
by this time so familiar, began again.
Or was it you who lowered me,
my arms already thrashing, the mineral
steam enfolding me? Mist on the balcony window,
the gray arabesques erasing everything.

# FIRE STORY

After the operation he'd wake
to drizzle that strained to lift itself
from the earth to the sky
the corner stop sign flashing its red
improbable signal
a message like
                    *d o ꞁ s*
his wife beside him asleep
The day before the bandages
were clipped away
his doctor warned him of this
                              that the eye
whose retina had been reattached
would see images as upside down
for months until his cells
instructed him that he was seeing otherwise
So they decided to vacation in the town
where they had met
a seaside resort
                    the off-season
a long recuperation
His wife read *Middlemarch* aloud
at night & he put out cigarettes
in an ashtray made of shell
They gathered mussels from the black
breakwater rocks where they hung
in clumps like castanets
                              growing
it seemed to him
downward from the sky
When they found the seal
fish still lodged in its mouth

**41**

trapped between the breakwater stones
he could not think of anything to say
though someone must have heard
its drowning cries as the tide returned
& confused them with the noise of gulls
*So simple*
                said his wife
*the details we discover about*
*ourselves too late to change our lives*

That night was the only time she told him the story

For several years before she met him
she had worked as the manager
of a record store
It was the recession
                        sales bad all over
& at her record chain's
annual meeting of managers
                              a Florida resort
a man wearing diamonds gold chains
lectured them on positive thinking
on turning fear into power
His methods at first were clumsy
a massage chain
                    two hundred record store managers
squatting in a skewed circle
to rub one another's backs
Then
        revival meeting call and response
until by midnight he had led
the crowd to a patch of beach
glowing with a bed of cinders ten feet long
He'd set up loudspeakers to play

the theme from *Rocky*
                    *Tonight is not*
said the gold chain man
*about walking on fire*
*It is a metaphor*
*for breaking through fear*
Now the first man ventures
tentatively to the edge
                    coals
hissing orange & sprints across
hurling himself into the crowd to announce
how easy it was & soon the woman
who years later will tell the story
has taken off her shoes
She closes her eyes & runs
falling to her knees at the end
before the months of pain
& skin grafts begin
hugging the man who had gone before

Stubbing her cigarette
the last sip of wine
she finishes
& he wants her to weep
                    to let him cup
her face in his hands though he knows that they
will never touch in innocence again
Turning her napkin
over & over
she says nothing more
He draws away his hand
                    willing

her face      & the candle flame      upright

**43**

# LES ENFANTS DU PARADIS

When the film breaks off
the mime Baptiste calls after
the carriage of Garance,

the only lover he has ever loved,
and the streets spill over
with a tide of white-faced revelers,

kinetic for the carnival.
Then I saw you in the row
behind, face bowed down,

avoiding mine,
both of us with others,
and the world swam back,

more plaintive than
the white face of Baptiste,
lost among the other faces,

Garance, diffident eyes,
the motion of her carriage—
images contrived

some forty years ago, too insistent
in their beauty. When you turned
I saw how they would enter

their separate lives, at last
resplendently heartless,
saw them each years later,

he at a restaurant table,
she at a *pensione* window,
trying to recall exactly

the moment so crucial
and utterly frail
even memory could break it.

# THE ANNIVERSARY

This must be the anniversary of the day
we woke to desert snow in October,
a vast beige quiet on the land.
And the woman on the foothill road
who'd swerved her red MG into a ditch
and now was weeping harshly enough
to make her voice the landscape's center.
You led her to the kitchen; I made coffee
and phoned the wreckers who wouldn't
drive up. Remember her face
in the coffee steam of the heatless house?
Too much talk about herself,
marriages, and daughters who had turned away,
facelifts and earlifts, embarrassing us
all morning to attention. *A hundred
years from now,* she said, *who
will know the difference?*—
a phrase my father used
years and half a continent away.
With valium and your electric blanket
she slept all afternoon on the sofa
while in the bedroom we made love
so softly we could hear the melting
snow above our breathing.
What I remember best is how in sleep
your hands would gesture to your dreams
until your dreams talked back
and laid them folded—delicate birds
pulsing on your breasts. We woke to find her gone,
a twenty dollar bill on the kitchen table.
Roads too slick, we turned back home
without the restaurant dinner it would buy.

45

Soup and tea for supper, and Monday
wreckers towed the red MG away. I used
the money for a California Chardonnay,
though the year was wrong, the taste
a little indistinct, and you pronounced it
*adequate, but hardly memorable*,
tracing my forehead in the lamplight.

gesture

# DATES, FOR EXAMPLE

*Handwritten annotations (right margin):*

moves from
the present—
noticing his
neighbor
to his neighbors
to his memories
book Hikmet to present date
meaning Lynda
to conjecture about
Hikmet
back to present
this neighbors
voice

Branches nodding in the fog,
   the trees are bruised with
      afternoon light. I'm watching

Phil Alexander next door
   stoop to a purple dahlia blossom
      larger than a hat. He brings us cukes,

late plum tomatoes, oxeye
   daisies in jars, recipes
      in a wavering hand

for kale soup and chowder. The gardener
   for Dos Passos and O'Neill, his anecdotes
      commence with roses, the Japanese elm

in O'Neill's yard, the way
   Dos Passos cut his lawn and hair—
      "A big man with a cowlick, he was.

Had the first power mower on the Cape."
   From my book by a Turkish poet
      I read, "Dates, for example,

are very important to Hikmet.
   The date of the poem
      is part of the poem itself."

It's the third of October, 1983,
   and I'm listening
      to Lynda's typewriter hesitantly clatter

the stanzas of a poem I would like
   Nazim Hikmet, twenty years dead this month,
      to read with approval

**49**

her hunched-down shoulders, under
   the shimmering, supernoval waterlilies
      of Monet's Giverny adorning her wall.

I want him to read her lines
   from his prison cell in Istanbul,
      exclaiming like a child when a phrase

seems right, saying *"This*
   would sound almost as good
      in Turkish!" Saying, "Woman,

your hair is a steady
   pulsing lily made of light!"
      He will talk with her this way

for hours. The plummeting sun disperses
   its light on the hundred masts
      of sloops and freighters

in the port of Istanbul below
   his window. It's evening now:
      the bars of the window marry

the first steady darkness until
   they seem to waver and disappear.
      Nazim Hikmet removes his glasses,

cups his hand around
   the single candle he's been issued this week.
      And Phil Alexander, with garden shears,

is pounding the doorframe behind me:
   *I brought you some rhubarb!*
      *I brought you some peppers!*

# THE BICYCLE

He held her as she wavered
  and grabbed tight to the handlebars,
    a woman in her fifties,

learning it for the first time,
  both of them, I was sure, in love.
    Watching like that, I thought

I knew nothing about love,
  nor how to be alone.
    All that spring he taught her

to coast awkwardly with him
  down their alley to the town pier
    where usually she fell.

Maybe then he kissed her,
  I can't remember.
    I went home. I didn't

believe in the bicycle
  or in Petrarch, who wanted love
    simple: moral and wounded. Always

this need for yearning and blame,
  and always there's a part of you
    giving unasked-for advice

because you think that everything
  believed in is betrayed.
    You fall until you get

the hang of it, and finally
  you have no wrath for anything,
    though you've still

discovered only
  the small, persistent skills
    you thought impossible to learn.

**51**

# THIS JOURNEY ON BACH'S BIRTHDAY

Finally sun, our red eyes gazing down at spring
beyond the train, fields not green, just diffuse.
The Little Fugue in G and "Jesu Joy" keep echoing
down the aisle. Bach's birthday: the Muse
on sloppy Muzak, all through Mississippi.
Still, we hum along. The gentle dead can soothe
so we read from the same book, *This Journey*
by James Wright. "In the end," you say, "he refused
the tragic." And today we at least
neglect it in the club car. We recite
James Wright to the astonished drunks, looking east
to Alabama, or maybe to the Italy of Wright
beyond, who gazes still at Verona in the rain.
There, beyond Ohio, the evening darkens into wine.

# PARTICULAR WORDS

*—for Richard Hugo*

Only once we spoke, this long distance about
the hyperbolic foreword to a book.
You wrote of someone almost me, but better.
Today, your death's a year and continent
away. Rain in torrents lathers the Cape,
the beaches shining out from mist until
you'd think we stood on Puget gazing West,

guessing the sunset's color. Now you're the past,
that's all. Now you're what we leave behind,
the way the sea leaves indiscriminate stones.
A fireplace and stairway waver above
the charred foundation of a lighthouse
and Coast Guard barracks. The stairway creaks
and feels drunk. On top you can bellow

your name to the salt spray until it echoes
back, or until your lungs get tired
and you stroll off to some house a mile
up the beach, a big man fumbling in
his raincoat for the key. So let's say
you come in drenched. Let's say I'm here
to meet you, a fifth of Jack, the fire going.

So now, at last, there's time for talk.
Naturally, there's some silence at first,
discomfort of strangers who've only met
in poems. But also my story of an honest
Minnesota ghost town called Hugo,
where I drove when someone phoned with the news.
Embarrassing, the photos I took:

the water tower flounders above lapsed
meadows with your name. The Gold Medal
grain mill glowers over a few sick elms.
It's wind, not drunks, that weaves the streets,
having traveled all night from Billings
and Bozeman, like distant cousins you'd rather
avoid. But you know the story: all towns

die the same, but come back different as lies
we tell to make each town more whole when lost.
Particular words get repeated for
effect: *Humiliation, Don't Come Back,
Remission, Death.* They write them in
to each town charter, honest lies we tell,
to soothe us, Dick, to give these sorrows form.

# PAST THE DARK ARROYO

Like a tourist with some phrases in the language
the sky is not a proper sky, too blue
for anyone. Nighttime will be cobalt,

with the salt of stars. And also particular,

the sky above St. David, Arizona, 1949.
Sundown, the horizon lucid for a moment,
looking for itself, and finding three figures

here on a car hood, lolling like saguaro arms.

They're resting with a canteen, a hundred miles to another town.
The heavy man, lighting a Viceroy, hand cupped lanternlike
for an instant before his face, is Pablo Neruda,

younger than we'll think of him in thirty years

as he puffs out from the book jackets, the red volcanic face
a little flabby. Two American communists,
one who used to write for Hollywood, have ferried Neruda

from the outskirts of El Paso, and by night

will move him north to Vancouver Island. He lifts
the flashlight, and writes in a yellow
spiral notebook: *cobalt with the salt of stars.*

He jokes with them—how night, enormous and American,

is now his only passport, though he tries too hard
to find the English words, and the men
know little Spanish. Past the dark arroyo,

he sees the whalebacks of mountains, a continent of exile,

some river gone wrong and zigzagging slowly north.
On the roadside, a sign banging hapless in the rising
Sonora wind: WHEN THE RAPTURE COMES, I WILL DEPART
THIS EARTH.
And Neruda, turning—*What is this to mean?*

# LITTLE ORGONON

The frail stalks of ocotillo
shimmer in the evening wind. The boy and father
weave their path up the foothill road,
the stars too tangible above them. The boy
calls his father *General,*
the father calls his child *Lieutenant.*
When the father opens the barbed wire gate
surrounding his death ray machine, a device
resembling a tulip or an antiaircraft gun,
he talks of summer nights in Vienna
and the days when he studied with Freud,
the sidewalk cafés on Alserstrasse,
cognac and espresso—*the city,*
*Lieutenant, had everything.*

Early November, and still the nights are warm.
The father removes his flannel shirt,
pours lemonade from a thermos. Together
they wait for the ghostly shapes
of UFOs to appear above the mesa, the bunkhouse
and laboratories of Little Orgonon.
The father believes
that alien beings intend to kill him,
and *Red Fascists* will discredit his discoveries.
Lately in his dreams, he finds himself
dead on a prison cell cot,
his body a leathery ball. And outside
a mud-colored rain that does not cease.

But tonight there is
no danger in the sky. Peering
through the death gun's sights,
they see only a few shaggy nimbus clouds,

57

so by midnight the father
is grumbling in German, waving his arms
the gesture he will use on the day
when Federal agents come to burn his books and papers
and the boy and his stepmother
are asked to help, lugging kerosene and alcohol
from the laboratory storeroom:
*It must be the smoke, Lieutenant,*
*bringing tears to my eyes.*

It's now very late. Orion the Hunter
has risen above Sonora's peaks. The stars
of his breastplate pulse white,
unspeakably hot. And this is the way
the boy for years will recall his father:
imperious and strange, face incandescent
in the gathering moonlight,

he stands to shake his fist at the sky.

# PENTECOST

Inside the cage, a card table with
a broken leg, an ancient Olivetti
and the bars etching stripes—
diagonal across the face of the man
who crouches there, a shell case
for a stool, talking to himself
in an English of his own design.
Writing in a spiral notebook, the kind
a child would take to school,
he tugs his beard's gray stubble.
This is Pisa, 1945.
Beyond the prison compound's barbed
wire mesh, twenty yards away, my father
in his corporal's stripes sips sick-
sweet grappa at a cafe with the men
of his platoon, the latticework canopy
intricately shadowing his face
as if he wore a beekeeper's veil.
He must wait ten days until a DC 3
can ferry him to the Azores;
then, a troop ship to Miami.
But until then he must help to guard
a compound for Italian prisoners
and spies, pacing the rows of tents
and cages every night from eight
until two. Some nights he smuggles
cigarettes and chocolates to the old man
who claims that he's American himself,
who speaks in whispers from within
the bars, in the corny mannered slang
of a movie cowboy. The old man
doesn't sleep, and sometimes all night

mumbles to himself as he rocks
on his cot, a blanket draped around
his shoulders. Another glass of grappa
and the afternoon appears to lift
its veil, awash in the white
piazza light. My father's friends
have left the table, and he takes out
pencil and paper to write down
the details of this light, its shimmer
on the whitewashed houses—a brilliance,
he thinks, in which the dead arise
to be born anew, and infinitely brighter
than the light he woke to
each morning through his bandages
that long month in Palermo, the Irish
nurse's cool hand on his shoulder.
He'll stare like this all afternoon.
And who could he write this to?
What is it he could say? He drops
his *lire* on the checkered tablecloth,
drains the glass, and blames
the trance of grappa for
the oddness of his thoughts—
how he felt, for a moment,
he'd had the power to speak in Greek,
Italian, and Chinese, his thoughts
churning forth in swirling cadences,
like oars striking brightly
against a sea so vivid
he's blinded, and must turn away.

Pentecost

**60**

# SHADOW GIRL

Below, the concrete bayou water leaps
along its strictures as I walk. Sunset,
and the joggers sway in profile against
the sky and onyx high-rise lights of Houston.
Side by side the next-door couple sprints
above the levee, flaunting their expensive
bodies, muscles rippling, oblivious grins
of self-regard. Sleek with perspiration,
they'll undress and make love in a dark

apartment, displaying their usual
shrill expertise. But later, the woman
will gaze awhile at the star quilt's clumsy
firmament, clothes flung like planets, straddling
the bed. How did she reach this place? I know
her longing can't be spoken. Call it secrecy,
neither recollection nor nostalgia.
Her husband twists and calls from sleep
robbing the air she breathes. She'll gaze

like this for hours. Last night in the airport's
strident fluorescent light, I watched your plane
climb east through clouds, our year-long separation
at midpoint now. I write tonight beyond
the muffled cries next door, remembering how
we strolled last year along the beaches
that composed your childhood, the creaking
boardwalk—amusement park shuttered for the season.
It reminded you of the final summer

61

before the Salk vaccine. July in New Jersey,
the beaches empty. Before sleep, you'd hear
the roller coaster's humming yellow scaffold
bulbs, the carousel silently revolving
its riderless horses. You were trying
to retrieve the smallest details of
those nights, the salt-air smell, the lighthouse arc
above you. Tonight, I know again how helplessly
we circle these separate childhoods,

sharing only marriage and the few
common gestures that the years have given,
how nights without you I wake to absence
almost palpable, how nights beside you
it's otherness I wake to, a secrecy
only partly mine, how marriage is
a pact with memory beyond ourselves.
It was twenty years ago: sure your parents
were asleep, you'd rise from the beach house cot,

unhinge the screen door hook, and walk all night
along the empty boardwalk. In the darkened
hall of mirrors you'd watch your vapory form,
afraid you were composed of only shadow,
a girl dancing feverish Ginger Rogers to prove
this image of herself could tell her something
magical. The girl picks up a shell and spins
its frail star in her hands. And in the mirror
the shadow girl answers back.

# THE WORLD OF DONALD EVANS

That light I was born to has kept itself
in place for many years. So childhood is remembered

as a sequence of mirrors and rooms, all leading
to where I bent over books of stamps

from countries whose names I couldn't pronounce.
Soon, I invented my own countries, and the stamps I issued,

the pages opening like rooms, explained me to myself,
until I saw myself as detail, color, and wash.

Beyond my window, three Dutch postmen
at a café table, stirring raw brown sugar

into coffee as I paint, the sky
an oyster color. If the world must always be

too private, too fervently imagined,
and hurts like the sun when it finally arrives

this afternoon in Amsterdam, our task
is to not shade our eyes. I wanted only

to make a small world visible—
*Katibo* and *Santor*, *Sabot* and *Stein*,

the names, you would think, of exotic roses,
opening now in a public garden, unfamiliar

with the sun. The habits and customs,
the literature and currency, a country so imagined

through stamps it continues without me.
Today, I paint a windmill

in a rainy country of windmills. With colored water
I paint the rain and year of a stamp

that never will be sent. And these postmen, grumbling,
rise from their table in a real rain,

unfolding ponchos, zipping pouches.
They wave to me, or do not wave.

The *why* of art, I wrote, and the *I give up*
of finding love or happiness. It is never,

I tell you, a matter of choice.
You go off toward the rain, delivering your letters.

Shadowless at 6:00 A.M., the houses spread
forward, the light percussive. Boarded shops,
and the season's first noreaster will gray
the sky all weekend. I leave you asleep

and jog for half an hour down Commercial
to the Truro line, the dog behind me
a breathless shadow. All morning she goes on
running in her sleep. Legs swim the paint-

flecked floor, the former owner's studio.
Yellow dragons snaking your kimono,
groggy you wake for coffee. And another
of the planet's final mornings begins.

Five years, ten, we'll carry ourselves
astonished into radiance as black
as the paintings lining the Rothko Chapel,
a thousand gradations of nothing.

I remember how you wept there last year
onto my shoulder, the stark relentless
octagon enveloping the bench
we stared from: cobalt-and-obsidian black,

silver black. So we paid our donation
to enter again our lives outside, the sullen
humidity of Houston. Now, half a continent away,
we've rented the house, 250 Bradford,

bought by Rothko in 1953, the year of my birth
and the eighth year of the nuclear bomb.
Last night on the blurry TV screen, an actor
playing Robert Oppenheimer strode

impatient to the Los Alamos bunker, his feet
raising minute cyclones of dust. The countdown,
the scientists arguing abstractedly
among themselves as Oppenheimer lifts

a chubby white Angora from her perch
on a cathode box, and lets her pink tongue
wander his arms and hands. We saw the firestorm
reflected in his sunglass mirrors, the wash

of color pressed against our faces
like the open palms of strangers.
But this morning, you sang Hank Williams
in the shower, reluctantly at first, then louder

and resplendently tuneless. The dog goes running
in her sleep. The cat in the maple slithers down
a saffron branch, the sparrow almost in reach.
And the morning again is luminous,

the smallest event the most elegiac.

# NOTES

"Dark-House Spearing"—an illegal icefishing technique.

"The Truth"—a monologue in response to Jarrell's poem of the same title. Jarrell's poem is spoken by the boy.

"Song of the Burning"—Jim Morrison, lead singer of The Doors, found dead in a Paris hotel room, 1971. Certain lines of the poem are inspired by Mayakovsky's final poem, "After One."

"The Anniversary"—the first line is taken from a poem by Keith Althaus.

*The World of Donald Evans*—the title of Willy Eisenhart's study of Evans, American painter who died in Amsterdam in 1975. His work consists of tiny paintings of stamps from imaginary countries.

"250 Bradford"—the Rothko chapel in Houston contains several large black murals from the final years of Rothko's career.

"This Moment" is for Christopher Buckley; "This Journey on Bach's Birthday" is for Richard Weaver; "Past the Dark Arroyo" is for Michael Bowden. Special thanks are also due the Yaddo and MacDowell colonies, The Centrum Foundation of Port Townsend, Washington, Richard Lyons, William Olsen, and Dave Jauss.

# PITT POETRY SERIES

**Ed Ochester, General Editor**

Dannie Abse, *Collected Poems*
Claribel Alegría, *Flowers from the Volcano*
Jon Anderson, *Death and Friends*
Jon Anderson, *In Sepia*
Jon Anderson, *Looking for Jonathan*
Maggie Anderson, *Cold Comfort*
John Balaban, *After Our War*
Michael Benedikt, *The Badminton at Great Barrington; Or, Gustave Mahler
   & the Chattanooga Choo-Choo*
Michael Burkard, *Ruby for Grief*
Kathy Callaway, *Heart of the Garfish*
Siv Cedering, *Letters from the Floating World*
Lorna Dee Cervantes, *Emplumada*
Robert Coles, *A Festering Sweetness: Poems of American People*
Kate Daniels, *The White Wave*
Norman Dubie, *Alehouse Sonnets*
Stuart Dybek, *Brass Knuckles*
Odysseus Elytis, *The Axion Esti*
Brendan Galvin, *The Minutes No One Owns*
Gary Gildner, *Blue Like the Heavens: New & Selected Poems*
Gary Gildner, *Digging for Indians*
Gary Gildner, *First Practice*
Gary Gildner, *Nails*
Gary Gildner, *The Runner*
Bruce Guernsey, *January Thaw*
Michael S. Harper, *Song: I Want a Witness*
Gwen Head, *The Ten Thousandth Night*
Barbara Helfgott Hyett, *In Evidence: Poems of the Liberation of Nazi
   Concentration Camps*
Milne Holton and Graham W. Reid, eds., *Reading the Ashes: An Anthology of
   the Poetry of Modern Macedonia*
Milne Holton and Paul Vangelisti, eds., *The New Polish Poetry: A Bilingual
   Collection*
David Huddle, *Paper Boy*
Lawrence Joseph, *Shouting at No One*
Shirley Kaufman, *From One Life to Another*
Shirley Kaufman, *Gold Country*
Etheridge Knight, *The Essential Etheridge Knight*
Ted Kooser, *One World at a Time*
Ted Kooser, *Sure Signs: New and Selected Poems*
Larry Levis, *Winter Stars*
Larry Levis, *Wrecking Crew*

Robert Louthan, *Living in Code*
Tom Lowenstein, tr., *Eskimo Poems from Canada and Greenland*
Archibald MacLeish, *The Great American Fourth of July Parade*
Peter Meinke, *Night Watch on the Chesapeake*
Peter Meinke, *Trying to Surprise God*
Judith Minty, *In the Presence of Mothers*
Carol Muske, *Camouflage*
Carol Muske, *Wyndmere*
Leonard Nathan, *Carrying On: New & Selected Poems*
Leonard Nathan, *Dear Blood*
Leonard Nathan, *Holding Patterns*
Kathleen Norris, *The Middle of the World*
Sharon Olds, *Satan Says*
Alicia Ostriker, *The Imaginary Lover*
Greg Pape, *Black Branches*
Greg Pape, *Border Crossings*
James Reiss, *Express*
William Pitt Root, *Faultdancing*
Liz Rosenberg, *The Fire Music*
Dennis Scott, *Uncle Time*
Herbert Scott, *Groceries*
Richard Shelton, *Of All the Dirty Words*
Richard Shelton, *Selected Poems, 1969-1981*
Richard Shelton, *You Can't Have Everything*
Arthur Smith, *Elegy on Independence Day*
Gary Soto, *Black Hair*
Gary Soto, *The Elements of San Joaquin*
Gary Soto, *The Tale of Sunlight*
Gary Soto, *Where Sparrows Work Hard*
Tomas Tranströmer, *Windows & Stones: Selected Poems*
Chase Twichell, *Northern Spy*
Chase Twichell, *The Odds*
Constance Urdang, *The Lone Woman and Others*
Constance Urdang, *Only the World*
Ronald Wallace, *People and Dog in the Sun*
Ronald Wallace, *Tunes for Bears to Dance To*
Cary Waterman, *The Salamander Migration and Other Poems*
Bruce Weigl, *A Romance*
David Wojahn, *Glassworks*
David P. Young, *The Names of a Hare in English*
Paul Zimmer, *Family Reunion: Selected and New Poems*

variety of voices, personae
comes to direct address - ends many poems this w
poem builds, one image on another
    yet weaves together - sometimes
    build in surprising ways

some rhetorical questions